HANDS-ON SCIENCE

NATURE

50 GREAT SCIENCE EXPERIMENTS AND PROJECTS

Consulting editor Chris Oxlade

southwater

This edition is published by Southwater

Southwater is an imprint of Anness Publishing Ltd
Hermes House, 88–89 Blackfriars Road, London SE1 8HA
tel. 020 7401 2077; fax 020 7633 9499;
www.southwaterbooks.com; info@anness.com

© Anness Publishing Ltd 2003

This edition distributed in the UK by The Manning Partnership Ltd
tel. 01225 478 444; fax 01225 478 440; sales@manning-partnership.co.uk

This edition distributed in the USA and Canada by National Book Network
tel. 301 459 3366; fax 301 459 1705; www.nbnbooks.com

This edition distributed in Australia by Pan Macmillan Australia
tel. 1300 135 113; fax 1300 135 103; customer.service@macmillan.com.au

This edition distributed in New Zealand by The Five Mile Press (NZ) Ltd
tel. (09) 444 4144; fax (09) 444 4518; fivemilenz@clear.net.nz

A CIP catalogue record for this book is available from the British Library.

Publisher: Joanna Lorenz
Managing Editor: Linda Fraser
Project Editor: Jennifer Schofield
Production Controller: Claire Rae
Designer: Axis Design Editions Ltd
Jacket Design: Dean Price
Contributing Authors: John Farndon, Jen Green, Robin Kerrod, Rodney Walshaw
Photographers: Paul Bricknell, John Freeman, Don Last, Robert Pickett, Tim Ridley
Illustrators: Cy Baker/Wildlife Art, Stephen Bennington, Peter Bull Art Studio, Stuart Carter,
Simon Gurr, Richard Hawke, Nick Hawken, Michael Lamb, Alan Male/Linden Artists,
Guy Smith, Clive Spong, Stephen Sweet/Simon Girling and Associates,
Alisa Tingley, John Whetton
Stylists: Ken Campbell, Jane Coney, Marion Elliot, Tim Grabham,
Thomasina Smith, Isolde Sommerfeldt, Melanie Williams

Previously published as part of a larger compendium, *150 Great Science Experiments*.

10 9 8 7 6 5 4 3 2 1

Publisher's Note

Picture Credits

b=bottom, t=top, c=centre, l=left, r=right

Bruce Coleman Ltd: 23cl. Frank Lane Picture Agency: 23bl, 32bl, 32bc, 32br. Nature Photographers Ltd: 12bc

Contents

Natural Wonders Close to Home

When forests are cut down, the plants and animal habitats that depend on the trees in those forests are put at risk. This book focuses on the natural habitats near your home to explore the importance of plants, insects and birds in the way nature works on Earth.

What is soil?

Soil is formed from decayed vegetable matter (dead leaves and plants), mineral grains and larger pieces of rock. Creatures, such as earthworms, help the decomposition process by mixing the soil. The process by which rocks are often broken down into smaller pieces is called weathering. Chemical weathering occurs when minerals are dissolved by water. Some minerals break down or dissolve quickly. Others, such as quartz, are not dissolved but stay behind in the soil as stones. The action of burrowing animals, insects and growing plants is called physical weathering. Attrition (grinding down) is another kind of physical weathering and occurs when wind-blown particles rub against each other. This kind of weathering occurs mainly in dry areas, such as deserts. You can see how attrition works simply by shaking some sugar cubes together in a glass jar.

In the first experiment, you can examine what makes up the soil. The second shows you the range of sizes of mineral and rock particles in a soil sample. In the last project, you can find out how sediments form in rivers, lakes and seas. First large and then finer particles of sediment are deposited.

▲ **On the horizon**
Soil occurs in layers, called horizons. There are four main horizons. The top horizon (also known as topsoil) is a layer of fine particles that supports the roots of plants and trees. The next two layers, beneath the topsoil, have larger soil particles. The bottom layer is partly solid rock.

Wormery

1 Cut the top off the large clear plastic bottle, as shown. Place the smaller bottle inside the larger one. Make sure the gap is evenly spaced all the way around the smaller bottle.

2 Fill the gap with layers of soil and sand to within 5cm of the top. Press the soil down lightly. Gently place the worms on top of the soil and cover them with rotting leaves.

3 Cover the sides with black paper. Keep the soil moist. After a few days, remove the paper to see how the worms have tunnelled away and dragged leaves into their burrows.

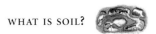

What is in soil?

1 Put on a pair of gardening gloves and place a trowel full of soil into the sieve. Shake the sieve over a piece of paper for about a minute or so.

2 Tap the side of the sieve gently to help separate the different parts of the soil. Are there bits that will not go through the sieve? Can you see if any of the bits are rock?

3 Use a magnifying glass to examine the soil particles that fall on to the paper. Are there any small creatures or mineral grains? Make a note of what you see in your notebook.

Big or small?

YOU WILL NEED

Wormery: large and small plastic bottles, scissors, funnel, gloves, damp soil, sand, six worms, rotting leaves, black paper, sticky tape.

What is in soil?: gloves, trowel, soil, sieve, paper, magnifying glass, notebook, pen.

Big or small?: scissors, large clear plastic bottle, wooden spoon, gravel, earth, sand, water, jug.

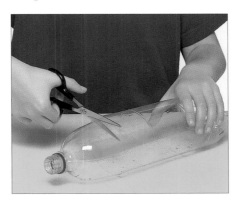

1 Use a pair of scissors to cut off the top of a large, clear plastic bottle. Ask an adult to help, if you need to. You can throw away the top part of the bottle.

floating soil and plant fragments

water made cloudy by fine particles of clay

settled mineral particles

2 Use a spoon to scoop some gravel, earth and sand into the bottom of the bottle. Add water to the mixture until it nearly reaches to the top of the bottle.

3 Stir vigorously to mix the stones, earth and sand with the water. In a river, soil and rock particles are mixed together and carried along by the moving water.

Leave the mixture to settle. You should find that the particles settle into different layers, with the heaviest particles at the bottom and the lightest at the top.

Examining soil

Beneath the ground, the soil teems with life. Worms, slugs, millipedes and beetles live there, feeding on decaying matter. Tiny living creatures, called decomposers, break down everything that remains. Decomposers include microscopic bacteria, fungi, woodlice, mites and small insects. They digest organic material such as dead animals, leaves and plants, and break it down into nutrients. This process, called decomposition, creates a rich fertilizer for plants growing in the soil. As organic material rots, its nutrients or goodness are returned to the soil. The nutrients dissolve in rain water and trickle down to tree and other plant roots below.

The first experiment demonstrates the best conditions for decomposing plants. It shows that plant material decays quickest in warm, moist areas. You can take a closer look at the decomposers themselves in the second project, which shows how to separate creepy-crawlies from the rotting leaves they live in. You could repeat the experiment with leaves from a different area and see if the insects you find are the same.

▲ **Feast for woodlice**
Rotting, in nature, does not happen by itself. Dead leaves are food for decomposers, such as woodlice. They eat the fallen leaves and pass many of the nutrients back into the soil, to be taken up again by the trees' roots.

Watching decay in the soil

YOU WILL NEED
gardening gloves, trowel (optional), two clean plastic containers, soil, dead leaves, water in a watering can, one container lid.

1 Be sure to wear a pair of gardening gloves for this project. Use your hand, or a trowel if you prefer, to fill two plastic containers with plenty of dry soil.

2 Put a layer of dead leaves on top of the soil in one of the containers. Water the leaves and soil thoroughly, then press the lid on to the container to cover it.

3 Place a layer of leaves on the dry soil in the other container. Do not water it and do not cover the container. Store both containers in a dry place.

After a few weeks, the leaves in the wet soil (*above left*) will have begun to rot, while those in the dry soil (*above right*) will have shrivelled.

Studying decomposers

YOU WILL NEED

plastic funnel, large clear jar, gloves, rotting leaves from a compost heap, black paper, sticky tape, desk lamp, magnifying glass, field guide.

1 Rotting leaves are covered in insects and other creepy-crawlies. You can separate them by using a lamp, a funnel and a large jar. Put the funnel inside the jar, as shown.

2 Wearing a pair of gardening gloves, loosely fill the funnel with rotting leaves. Tape a sheet of black paper around the sides of the jar to block out the light.

3 Place the lamp so that it shines on to the leaves. The creatures will move away from the heat and light of the lamp and fall down the slippery funnel into the jar below.

After an hour, there will be several creatures in the jar. Look at them with a magnifying glass and use a field guide to identify them. Then return the creatures to where you found them.

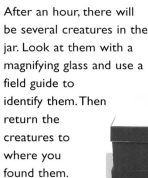

Tree study

There are several kinds of trees. In tropical rainforests, where it is warm and wet all year, most trees are evergreen and keep their leaves all year round. Tropical rainforests are found near the Equator, where there is little difference between the seasons. In countries with a temperate (moderate) climate, deciduous, broad-leaved trees shed their leaves in autumn. Losing leaves reduces evaporation. This helps the tree conserve energy and water when the ground water is frozen, and reduces damage by frost.

Trees can be identified by looking at such characteristics as bark, leaves and flowers, and in autumn by their fruits and nuts, some of which are shown on the right. The size and shape of the trunk and branches can also help to identify a tree, and scientists record the tree's girth by measuring the distance around the trunk at chest height. You can study trees in your garden, a local park or wood following the same checks. Choose an area of mixed woodland with many different trees. Always remember to take an adult with you to keep you safe.

leaf from a plane tree

seedcase from a sycamore tree

hips and leaves from a cockspur thorn tree

a chestnut and its case from a horse chestnut tree

seeds from a lime tree

acorn and its cup from an oak tree

Identifying trees

1 Walk along a path in your chosen area. Try to identify the trees you find there from their general height and shape. Use a field guide to help you.

2 Bark can help you identify some trees. Silver birch bark is smooth and white with dark cracks. Match the bark of different trees with pictures in your guide.

3 Study leaf colours and shapes, and the fruits and seeds of trees. Learn to identify trees with the help of the field guide, and make a record of them in a notebook.

Measuring a tree's height

1 With the metre rule, measure 19m from the tree and push the stick into the ground. Measure another metre from the stick and lie down straight on the ground.

2 Use one eye to line up the top of the tree with the stick. Get a friend to mark this point on the stick in the ground. The height of the tree is 20 times this distance.

Measuring a tree's girth

1 Stick a piece of tape on the end of a piece of string. Wrap the string around a tree trunk at chest height. Mark where it meets the tape with your finger.

2 Lay the string along the ruler to find the length. This figure is the girth of the tree. Measure another tree of the same species. Is its girth the same? Why might they differ?

	1 square = 2.5cm
evergreen	
beech	
horse chestnut	
cherry	
silverbirch	

3 Make a chart with drawings of the different trees that you have measured. The trees with the thickest trunks are usually older than those with slender trunks.

▲ **Rings of age**
You can clearly see the growth rings on the trunk of this old oak tree. Each year the tree grows a new ring of wood just under the bark.

Looking at bark

▲ Close-up view

If you look closely at the bark of a tree you can discover many clues about its life. Plants and fungi may be clinging to the surface. There might also be insects and other tiny creatures hiding inside cracks.

YOU WILL NEED

magnifying glass, field guide,

notebook, pencil.

Become a bark detective

The skin that covers a tree – the bark – keeps the tree from drying out and helps to protect it against attack by animals and fungi. Bark may be thin and smooth or thick and knobbly, depending on the type of tree and its age. Young trees usually have smooth bark on their trunks and branches. Old bark stretches and cracks or peels as the trunk grows wider year by year. Just underneath the bark is a delicate layer of tissue called a phloem. It carries nutrients from the leaves to all parts of the tree. If a bark is damaged all around the tree trunk, the flow of food stops and the tree dies.

The appearance of the bark can help you decide what species (type) a tree is. Different trees have different kinds of bark. A mature beech tree has smooth, thin bark that is about 1cm deep. A redwood tree of the same size has hairy, fibrous bark that is up to 15cm thick. Many conifers, such as pines and spruces, have bark that flakes off. Follow the first two projects and become a bark detective by studying the bark up close and making a collection of your own bark rubbings. The third project will help you estimate the size of a tree.

1 Bark does not stretch, but cracks and peels as a tree grows. Use a magnifying glass to search in the cracks during spring and summer for tiny insects and other creatures.

2 The bark has fallen away from this dead tree revealing the holes chewed by beetle grubs underneath. Some grubs live under the bark for several years.

3 Where the bark is damp, you will often find powdery green patches. These are millions of microscopic plants called algae that live side by side on the bark's surface.

Bark rubbing book

YOU WILL NEED

paper, wax crayons, pencil, coloured

card, bradawl or hole puncher,

ribbon, adhesive.

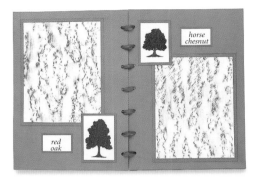

1 Ask a friend to hold a sheet of paper steady against the bark. Rub the side of a crayon over the paper with long, even strokes. Write the name of the tree beside each rubbing.

2 Punch holes into pieces of coloured card and link them with ribbon. Stick your rubbings on to each page. You could include a silhouette of each tree as well.

Measuring the crown

YOU WILL NEED

compass, marker, metre

ruler, squared paper, ruler,

coloured pencils.

1 Using the compass, walk away from the tree towards north. Ask a friend to call out when you reach the edge of the area covered by the leaves. Place a marker at this point.

2 Repeat for the other seven main compass directions (NE, E, SE, S, SW, W, NW). Measure the distances back to the trunk with a metre ruler and note them down.

3 Plot your results on a piece of squared paper. Measure 1cm on the paper for each metre on the ground. Draw lines from the centre of the paper, for each compass direction.

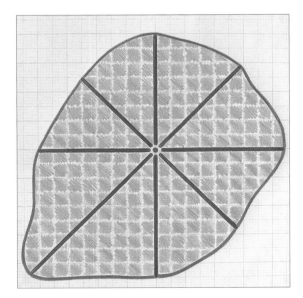

What you have sketched and coloured in shows the shape of the area covered by trees leaves and branches (the crown). Count the squares and half squares to find the size of the area of the crown. Do not count part-squares if they are less than a half. Each 1cm square represents 1m. Compare with other trees in the area. Generally, the older the tree, the more likely it will have a larger crown.

Specimen collection

Different kinds of trees grow naturally in different parts of the world. Where they grow depends mainly on climate. Look closely at trees in winter and you will see that even deciduous trees are not completely bare. Each twig has buds along its sides and at the tip. Buds have protective skins with tiny immature leaves and stems curled up inside. When spring sunshine warms the trees, buds begin to grow and swell. Finally they burst open and small leaves emerge. Leaves contain pipes called veins. Water pumps into these veins, making the leaves stiffen and flatten as they grow to full size.

To learn about trees, you can make a collection of dead leaves, cones and bark from each one you study. Do not forget to look for things throughout the year – flowers and buds in spring, seeds and fruit in autumn. Label your collection.

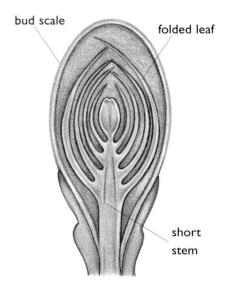

bud scale

folded leaf

short stem

▲ Budding

Buds grow in the centre of a twig between two leaf stems. An unopened bud contains tiny leaves and a shoot that will grow in spring and make the leaf stem longer. The illustration above shows what it looks like inside.

Tree zones

Evergreen conifer trees, such as pine and firs, usually grow where the climate is cold. Long snowy winters are followed by short cool summers, with moderate amounts of rain. Forests of conifers grow in a band across North America, Europe and Asia.

Broad-leaved deciduous trees, such as oak, ash and maple, grow in temperate climates away from hot, dry tropics or the snowy poles. There are more kinds of trees than in a coniferous forest. Temperate forests are found in North America, Europe, Asia and New Zealand.

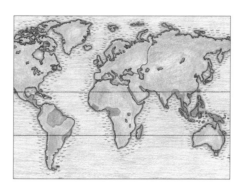

Tropical countries lie close to the Equator. The weather is hot and daylight lasts for 12 hours a day for most of the year. Dense rainforests grow where heavy rain falls almost continuously, such as South America, Africa, Asia and Australasia.

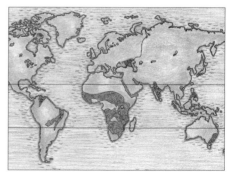

Savanna is a dry, tropical grassland, with some shrubs and bushes. Trees grow alone or in widely spaced small groups. Forests cannot grow because the dry season lasts most of the year. Trees that do grow here are species that can survive for long periods without water.

Collecting specimens

1 How many different leaves and cones can you find? Make sure you note down the name of the tree that each specimen comes from. Start a collection with your friends.

2 To dry and flatten your leaves, place sheets of kitchen paper between the pages of a large and heavy book. Lay your leaves out on the paper on one side only. Close the book.

3 Pile more books on top. Make sure the pile cannot topple over and will not get disturbed. The weight presses the leaves flat while the kitchen paper absorbs moisture.

4 Wait for at least one month until the leaves are flat and dry. Glue them into your notebook or on to sheets of thick paper and make them into a book. Use a field guide to identify each leaf.

5 For bark specimens, only collect bark from dead trees that have fallen over. You can make bark rubbings from living trees. See page 12 for instructions on how to make rubbings.

6 Springtime flowers soon wither and die. These young horse chestnut conkers will last much longer. It is better to take photographs of flowers rather than pick them.

7 You can look at young cones and leaves from the lowest branches of evergreen pines, firs and cedars. Look under these trees for cones that have fallen.

Make a large display case for your collection. You can make this from a shoe box by sticking in pieces of card to make compartments. Pressed leaves keep their shape and can last for a long time, if they are kept dry.

How plants grow

All plants need water to live. They do not take in food as animals do, but make their own using water from the ground and carbon dioxide gas from the air. Water is absorbed through a plant's roots. It travels up through the stem or trunk and on to the leaves, shoots and flowers. The water also carries the nutrients from the soil to all parts of the plant. In the leaves, nutrients and water are used for photosynthesis, the process of making energy from light. Excess water not needed by the plant evaporates back into the air in the form of water vapour in a process called transpiration. You can see how much water vapour is transpired by a plant in the first experiment.

When a seed begins to grow we say that it has germinated. Germination occurs when conditions are warm and moist enough for the seed to swell and split its skin. A tiny root grows downwards and a thin shoot pushes upwards towards the light. The second project shows you how to germinate a seed and help it grow into a tree. Germinating a seed in this way takes about two months.

leaves absorb carbon dioxide and release oxygen though tiny holes on their undersides

chlorophyll in leaves combines carbon dioxide gas and water to make glucose and oxygen

energy is absorbed from the Sun on the top sides of the leaves

roots take in water and minerals

▲ Converting energy

Photosynthesis is the process through which plants use the water in the ground and the energy in sunlight to make their food. Leaves take in carbon dioxide and water to make oxygen and glucose (sugar). Glucose flows to all parts of the plant, supplying energy for growth. Oxygen gas escapes through the holes on the underside of the leaves. The oxygen is released back into the air. We need oxygen to breathe.

Survival in the wetlands ▶

Swamps are places where the ground is permanently waterlogged, such as in muddy river estuaries. Most trees cannot survive in swamps because they need fresh water and air around their roots. Some types of mangroves have breathing roots that grow upwards so that their tips are above the surface of the water. Mangrove swamps are home to kingfishers, giant water bugs, crabs, turtles, crocodiles and mudskippers, a type of fish that spends much of its time out of water.

Evaporation in action

YOU WILL NEED

Evaporation in action: house plant, watering can, clear plastic bag, sticky tape, scissors.

Germinate an acorn: 10cm (diameter) flower pot, compost, gloves, acorns or another tree's seeds, trowel, watering can.

1 Water the house plant well using a watering can. Water the plant at the base so the roots can draw the water up. If you water the plant from the top, water just the soil not the plant itself.

2 Place a large, transparent plastic bag over the plant, taking care not to damage the leaves. Tape the bag tightly around the pot. Leave the plant overnight.

◄ Floating water

Trees pass millions of litres of water vapour into the air each day. The vapour forms thick clouds of tiny water droplets over the forest.

3 Have a look at the plant the next day. Inside the bag, water vapour given off by the plant turns back into water. The air inside is warm and moist, like the air in a rainforest.

Germinate an acorn

1 Fill the flower pot with compost and bury an acorn just beneath the surface. Put it in a warm place and keep the soil moist. Plant several acorns, as one may not germinate.

2 When a tiny tree starts to grow by itself, it is called a seedling. It needs light and regular watering to grow well. Do not soak the soil with water or the roots will rot and die.

3 Your seedling should grow rapidly for a few weeks and then stop. During winter it will need little water. In spring you can remove the seedling from its pot and plant it outside.

Reaching for light

Look at a leaf and you will see that the top side is usually greener than the underside. This is because there is more chlorophyll, a green substance that traps energy from sunlight. Plants cannot move around to find food as animals do. Instead, they make their own. The green cells work like tiny solar panels, using sunlight to combine carbon dioxide gas from the air and water from the ground. The cells then produce a sugar (glucose) and oxygen gas. This process is called photosynthesis. Without light, plants cannot make their food.

Photosynthesis is the ultimate source of food on Earth, because animals eat plants or other animals that live on plants. Photosynthesis is also the source of all oxygen in our atmosphere. The projects show how plants try to reach the light. Epiphytes are special kinds of plants that do not need to grow in soil. They live on high branches in the rainforests to get closer to the light.

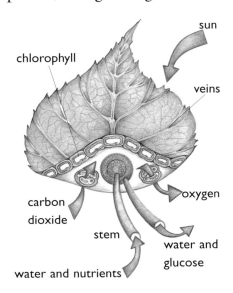

▲ Making energy
Photosynthesis happens near the top surface of a leaf where sunlight has the strongest impact.

▲ Catching the rays
Trees spread their leaves widely to absorb as much energy as they can from sunlight. They use the energy to make a sugary substance called glucose. Liquids flow in and out of leaves through veins. Veins also act like ribs that help to stiffen the leaf and keep it flat.

Grow your own epiphyte

1 Put on a pair of gloves. Wrap moss around one end of the branch or a piece of driftwood. Tie the moss securely in place with cotton thread.

2 Pile some gravel into a sturdy plant pot until the pot is almost full. It needs to be almost full to support the wood. You could use a trowel to help you transfer the gravel.

3 Now push the branch or driftwood down into the gravel, until it stands up in the pot without tipping it over. Use a water spray to spray the moss with water.

4 Arrange the epiphytes (available from garden centres) by pressing them gently into the moss. A drop of glue on the base of each plant will help hold it in place.

5 Remember to spray the epiphytes from time to time with water. You could also add few drops of liquid plant food to help the epiphytes to grow.

Epiphytes grow well indoors and make an unusual display. They do not need soil to grow. Instead they wrap their roots around a branch.

Searching for the light

YOU WILL NEED

Grow your own epiphyte:

gardening gloves, sphagnum moss, branch or drfitwood, cotton thread, gravel, plant pot, trowel, water spray, epiphytes, glue, liquid plant food.

Searching for the light: shoe box, scissors, stiff card, sticky tape, black paint, paintbrush, gardening gloves, runner bean, plant pot, compost, water.

1 Watch a plant search for the light as it grows, by making a maze. Cut a hole in the end of a shoe box and stick eight flaps of card inside with sticky tape, as shown here.

2 Paint the inside of the box and lid black all over. The black paint will stop the light that enters through the hole from being reflected around inside the box.

3 Wearing gloves, plant a runner bean in a small pot of compost. Water the soil each day to keep it moist, but not too wet. Some days, no water may be needed.

4 When the plant has a shoot, stand it at the bottom of your maze. Close the lid and place the maze in a sunny spot. Once a day, remove the lid to see if the seedling needs watering.

The plant will find its way through the maze as it steadily moves towards the light. Eventually it will poke out through the hole at the top of the shoe box.

Natural water pumps

When you look at a tree, you only see a part of it. Unseen roots spread out underground as wide as the branches above. These roots anchor a tree in the ground and hold it up against the force of the wind. Roots also help the tree to grow by taking up water and nutrients from the soil through the trunk to the leaves. Trees act like a natural pump – many trees over 50m tall pump hundreds of litres of water a day in order to grow. You can suck a drink up through a straw, but trees cannot do this. They use a method called osmosis to draw the water upwards. The first experiment shows how osmosis works. Water inside the roots (sap) has a higher concentration of sugar than the water outside. The process of osmosis draws water from the soil, where the concentration is low, to inside the root, where concentration is high.

The second experiment uses coloured water to show how water actually travels up a plant's root. All living things are made up of little units called cells. Water can travel through cell walls but sugars cannot. During osmosis, water always moves in a set direction – from the side where there is less sugar dissolved in it to the side where there is more.

▲ **Suck it and see**
To find out how difficult it is to suck up water, carefully join together straws with sticky tape. The longer the straw, the more difficult it is for you to suck up the drink. The best mechanical pumps can only manage 10m.

How osmosis works

YOU WILL NEED
large potato, ruler, chopping board, peeler, knife, teaspoon, two shallow dishes, water, sugar.

1 You will need a large, smooth potato about 10cm long and 6cm across. Carefully peel the potato over a chopping board to protect the work surface.

2 Cut the peeled potato in half and then slice off the rounded ends. You will now have two round potato slices. Each slice should be about 3cm thick.

3 Use a teaspoon to scoop out a hollow in each potato slice. Place each slice in its own shallow dish and fill the dishes with water to about 1cm in depth.

4 Half fill both hollows with water. Add ½ tsp of sugar to one hollow. Cover and leave the potatoes for one day. (*Dye has been added to the water here to make it show up.*)

5 The level of liquid in the sugary hollow has risen. Osmosis has made more water move into this potato from the dish. The level in the other potato has not risen.

Osmosis in colour

YOU WILL NEED

water, two tall drinking glasses, water-soluble ink or food dye, white carnation, scissors, sticky tape.

1 Pour some water into two tall drinking glasses. Add a few drops of ink or food dye to one of the glasses to give the water a strong, bright colour.

2 Use scissors to split the stem of the carnation lengthwise to about half way up the stem. Bind the stem with tape so that it does not split any further.

3 Place the glasses side by side on a windowsill, and stand one half of the stem in each glass. Lean the flower against the window if it will not stand up on its own.

4 After a few hours, check to see what has happened. One half of the flower will be coloured with the dye. The other half of the flower will have remained white.

Coloured water is drawn up one side of the split stem. The petals on that side of the flower have turned pink.

Seeds and plant life

Most plants reproduce by making seeds, which sprout and grow into new plants. To produce seeds, plants must be fertilized by pollen, usually from another plant of the same species (kind). Many plants rely on insects such as bees and butterflies to spread pollen. Seeds are mostly spread by animals that eat the fruit produced by plants, and by wind. In some plants, such as those in rainforests, seeds may also be carried by water. The plants in your local area disperse (spread) their seeds in these ways, too. In the company of an adult, you can survey the seeds and plants in your local wood.

YOU WILL NEED

eight pegs, metre ruler or tape measure, string, field guide, pen, notebook, coloured pencils and pens, graph paper.

Carrying out a plant survey

1 Choose a patch of ground to sample and put in a peg. Measure 1m with the ruler and put in another peg. Stretch and tie a piece of string between the pegs.

2 Now measure the remaining sides, pushing in two more pegs and stretching and tying string between them to mark out one square metre.

3 Measure and mark the midpoint of each piece of stretched string with pegs. Stretch more string between these pegs to divide the square into quarters.

4 Use your field guide to help you to identify the plant species growing in each quarter of the square. Do different plants or the same ones grow in each area?

5 Draw a chart on graph paper to record each plant's position. Use different colours for each plant type that you found. Add up the total number of each type of plant.

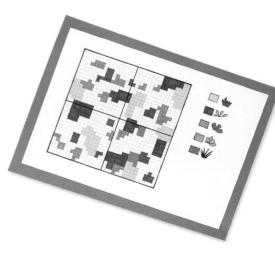

Looking at seed dispersal

1 Look out for nibbled nuts and acorns. These seeds are food for many animals. Collect seeds in a pot, cover with muslin and secure with an elastic band.

2 Visit your local pond or stream to find seeds, such as alders, that are dispersed by water. Use your field guide to identify any seeds you see floating on the water.

3 Maple and sycamore trees have light seeds with wings. As they fall, the wings spin the seed through the air, helping it to fly farther and germinate far from the parent tree.

4 Find a dandelion clock. Plants such as dandelions have very light seeds, each with its own small parachute of fine threads. These are carried away by the wind.

5 Look for the seed capsules of poppies. They are like pepper pots with hundreds of tiny seeds inside. As the wind shakes the capsule, the seeds burst out and scatter widely.

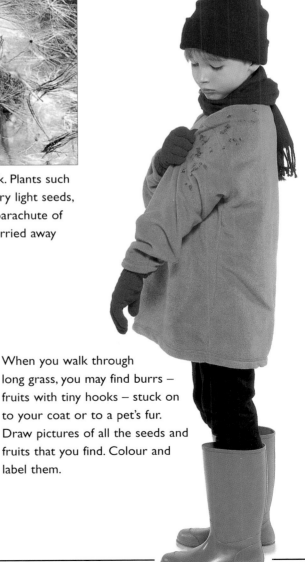

When you walk through long grass, you may find burrs – fruits with tiny hooks – stuck on to your coat or to a pet's fur. Draw pictures of all the seeds and fruits that you find. Colour and label them.

Growing from fruit

There are many kinds of fruits grown in the garden. Some fruits are soft, such as apples and oranges, and others are hard such as acorns and walnuts. Even tough little hawthorn berries and sycamore wings are fruits. Fruits all have seeds protected inside a container. The container may be the soft flesh of a plum or the hard shell of a hazelnut. You can find out the seeds inside different fruits. Some examples are given here. If you want to try others, use fruits bought from your local grocery store since some wild berries are poisonous.

orange   apple

plum

lemon

apricot

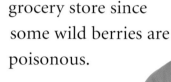

◄ **Centre spot**

These fruits are soft, fleshy and sweet. Like most fruits, they have grown from the reproductive ovaries inside female flowers. Open any fruit and inside you will find seeds.

Looking at apple seeds

1 Cut open an apple with a sharp knife. Inside you will find several brown seeds, or pips, in the centre. Use the tweezers to remove as many of the seeds as you want.

2 Use the tweezers to carefully remove the soft outer skin of a seed. Underneath the skin you will find the slippery white seed. Treat it carefully – it is very delicate.

3 Look under a magnifier to see the embryo (at the tip). The rest of the seed is the cotyledon, which provides food so the embryo will grow into a new root and shoot.

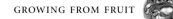

Looking inside a nut

1 Nuts are fruits that have their seeds inside a hard shell. Carefully crack open a hazelnut with a pair of nutcrackers and look for the nut kernel (seed) inside.

2 Use scissors to scrape off the dark outer skin from the kernel. You should then be able to separate the white hazelnut into two halves. Look at these with a magnifying glass.

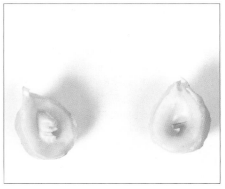

3 Inside the nut is a tiny embryo. This part grows into roots and a stem. The two larger parts are the cotyledons, which supply energy for the sprouting seed to grow.

How a seed grows

1 Curl blotting paper inside a jar. Push a bean seed halfway down between the paper and the glass. Add water to a depth of 2cm and stand the jar in a light, warm place.

2 When the seed germinates, you will see the root growing downwards. Turn the jar so that the root points to the right. What do you think will happen?

As the root continues to grow, it changes direction so that it is growing downwards again.

Tropical seeds

1 An avocado stone is the seed of the avocado plant. Clean off any flesh left on the stone and then carefully push three cocktail sticks into the stone, as shown above.

2 Fill a jar with water and suspend the stone so that it just touches the waterline. Keep the jar in a warm, shady place and top up the water regularly.

3 When roots begin to grow downwards, plant the stone in a pot filled with compost. Place the pot where the air is warm and humid and wait for your seedling to grow.

Life in the forest

People who live in forests build their homes from materials found in the forest. In South America, the Yanomami tribe's large, round huts are made with trees bent into a dome shape, lashed with vines and thatched with palm leaves. The Yanomami sleep on the roof in hammocks made of woven grasses, slung from the rafters. Scientists working in rainforests sometimes build temporary shelters with branches. You can build a shelter by following these instructions, but you may need the help of an adult. When looking for branches to make your shelter with, take an adult with you. Collect the branches from your garden or a public area. Do not cut them from trees – always gather them from the ground, where they have fallen naturally.

YOU WILL NEED

five sturdy branches, rope or thick string, a friend or adult to help, guy-ropes or strings, eight pegs, tarpaulin, ground sheet, two poles.

▲ Temperate forests

Beech, ash and oak grow in this northern European forest. Birds and squirrels live in the trees. Bluebells and wood anemones grow on the forest floor. Worms, moles and badgers burrow underground. Larger animals include deer, wild pigs and bears.

▲ Conifer forests

Hemlocks, cypresses and giant redwoods grow in conifer forests in North America. Woodpeckers and chipmunks search for food in the trees. Ferns grow on the forest floor. Moose and beavers live near lakes and black bears scavenge for food.

▲ Trees in the savanna

The African savanna is dotted with drought-resistant trees, such as baobabs (bottle trees), and acacias. Herds of zebra, antelope and gazelles feed on grass. Taller giraffes and elephants can reach up into the trees for fresh leaves.

▲ Tropical rainforest

Many trees and climbing plants live in tropical rainforests such as the Amazon of South America. Monkeys and brightly coloured birds live high up in the trees, where there is light and food. Dense rotting vegetation covers the ground.

Build a shelter

1 Lash the ends of two sturdy branches together with rope or string. Stand the branches upright to make an A-frame. You could tie the A-frame to a tree for extra support.

2 Lash two more branches together. Stand them upright about 2m from the first A-frame. Place a lighter branch on top to make a ridge pole and lash it in place.

3 Attach two guy-ropes or strings to each of the A-frames and peg the guy-ropes securely into the ground. Now throw a tarpaulin over the ridge pole to form the roof.

4 Attach guy-ropes or strings to eyeholes in the corners of the tarpaulin and peg them securely into the ground. Stretch the tarpaulin tight to make the roof.

5 Thread string through the eyeholes on opposite sides of the ground sheet to make the sheet into a sort of tube. Push two poles inside the sheet, one on each side.

6 Pull the two poles apart to make a stretcher shape that will fit inside the shelter. This will form the hammock so that you will be able to rest off the ground.

7 Wedge the stretcher inside your shelter, so that the poles rest on the outside of the upright A-frames. Make sure your hammock is secure and will not slip down the poles.

Now it's time to try out your hammock and take a well-earned rest!

Soil erosion

All around the world, rainforests are being cut down at an alarming rate. At the beginning of the 1900s, tropical forests covered about twice the area they do today. Experts estimate that an area of rainforest about the size of England is lost each year. One of the main reasons for this is logging – the felling of trees for timber. Many rainforest trees are made of valuable hardwoods, such as teak and mahogany, which are used for building houses and making furniture. Trees are also cleared to create roads and new pasture for cattle.

The roots of trees and other plants help to hold forest soil together. When the trees are felled, the soil is left bare. In heavy rainfall, the earth is washed away, just as it is in the first project. However, when forests are left alone, they sustain themselves indefinitely, recycling water and nutrients from the soil. You can see how this works by growing a mini-jungle. The bottle or jar reproduces the warm, moist conditions and constant high temperatures of a rainforest. The plants recycle their own moisture so they rarely need watering.

▲ **Vanishing forests**

This illustration shows the effects of deforestation. Tree roots help to hold the soil in place and leaves absorb the force of falling rain. When forests are cut down, soil is washed away and exposed earth dries up and hardens.

YOU WILL NEED

potted plant, two plastic cups, plant pot, compost or soil, two watering cans.

Looking at soil erosion

1 Fit the potted plant into the neck of one of the plastic cups. Fill the empty plant pot with compost or soil. Place the pot into the neck of the other plastic cup.

2 Pour water on to the potted plant and into the pot of soil. What happens? You will find that water passes more quickly through the pot without the plant.

Water passing through the pot without the plant is muddy because more soil has been washed through. Water passes more slowly through the pot with the plant. It will trickle through almost clear.

Plant a mini-jungle

YOU WILL NEED

large plastic bottle or jar with a lid, gloves, gravel, charcoal, potting compost, spoon or trowel, small tropical plants, plant sprayer or watering can with sprinkler rose.

1 Wash out your bottle or jar to make sure it is clean. Place handfuls of gravel into the bottom of the bottle, to make the lowest layer of the mini-jungle.

2 Mix a little charcoal with the potting compost. Add a deep layer of compost mixture on top of the gravel and then smooth out the soil so that it is level.

3 Make some quite large holes for the plants in the soil with a spoon or trowel. Then gently lift the plants out of their pots and lower them into the holes you have made.

4 Firm the soil down around the base of each plant. You can use a spoon or a trowel to do this if you find it difficult to reach that far with your fingers.

5 Mist the plants and soil quite thoroughly with water from a plant sprayer, or using a watering can with a sprinkler attachment. This is your tropical rain!

6 Put the lid on the bottle or jar, and your mini-jungle is complete. The water you have sprayed is recycled inside the bottle or jar, so you will not need to water your jungle often. Moisture from the plants condenses on the sides of the bottle or jar. It will then drip down into the soil, to be reused.

The balance of life

Life on Earth is a vast jigsaw of plant and animal activity. The world can be split into vegetation regions according to the kind of plants that thrive there. Scientists often break down the vegetation regions into smaller units, such as tropical rainforests or freshwater lakes. They might go further to identify individual trees or a pond. Each unit, where the creatures living there interact with each other, is called an ecosystem.

An ecosystem is a community of living things, or organisms, that all depend on each other. An aquarium like the one in the project is a miniature freshwater ecosystem. All plants need particular conditions of soil and climate to survive. Animals also survive by adapting to and interacting with their surroundings and the local climate.

If a particular species from an ecosystem is removed, the existence of other living things is threatened. If the plants on which a certain caterpillar feeds are destroyed, the caterpillars die. Eventually, the birds that feed on the caterpillars and the foxes that feed on the birds would starve.

▲ Building an ecosystem

When there is enough warmth and moisture in an area of bare, rocky land, simple plants grow. The first to take hold are mosses and lichens. They are followed by tough grasses, which hold the soil together. As they die and rot, they add nutrients to the soil, preparing it for bigger plants to grow. Soon there is enough to support small shrubs and tough trees, such as pines, and eventually deciduous trees such as oaks. This process is called vegetation succession. It would take about 200 years for deciduous woodland to evolve from the moss and lichen stage.

Feeding habits ▸

Humans and animals depend on other living things for food. This picture shows how this food chain or web works. A grasshopper eats a leaf of grass, a thrush may eat the grasshopper and a kestrel may eat the thrush. When the kestrel dies, bacteria break its body down and add nutrients to the soil so that new plants can grow. Herbivorous animals eat plants only. Carnivores are meat eaters, and omnivores eat both animals and plants. Plants make their own food from sunlight, and so are called autotrophs (self-feeders).

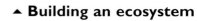

Make your own aquarium ecosystem

YOU WILL NEED

gravel, net, plastic bowl, jug, water, aquarium tank, rocks and pieces of wood, water plants, pondwater, water animals.

1 Put the gravel in a net. Rinse it in a plastic bowl of water or run it under the cold water tap in the sink. This will discourage the formation of green algae.

2 Spread the gravel unevenly over base of the tank to a depth of about 3cm. Add rocks and pieces of wood. These give surfaces for snails to feed on.

3 Fill the tank to about the halfway mark with tap water. Pour the water gently from a jug to avoid disturbing the landscape and churning up the gravel.

4 Add some water plants from an aquarium centre. Keep some of them in their pots, but take the others out gently. Then root them in the gravel.

5 Now add a jugful of pondwater. This will contain organisms, such as daphnia (water fleas), which add to the life of your aquarium. You can buy pondwater in a garden centre.

6 Add a few water animals you have collected from local ponds, such as tadpoles in frog spawn or water snails. Take care not to overcrowd the aquarium.

7 Place the tank in bright light, but not in direct sunlight. You can watch the plants in the tank grow. Keep the water clean by removing dead matter off the gravel every few weeks.

Animal tracks and footprints

Wild creatures in the forest usually run away when humans approach. However, you can learn a lot about birds and other animals by looking at their tracks. You could go to a wood with an adult to hunt for animal tracks in soft or wet ground. The banks of streams and rivers are often criss-crossed by prints from animals who have gone there to drink.

Different groups of animals (mammals, birds, reptiles and amphibians) leave different tracks. The first project shows you how to look for these prints. Tracks give clues about the size and weight of the animal. They also show how animals move – whether they run, hop, slide or slither. Large, heavy birds for example, such as geese, waddle along – shifting their weight from side to side. Their prints show that they place one foot in front of the other and slightly to the side, rather like the way humans walk. Small birds, such as tits and finches, hop along on thin legs and feet. They leave tracks of tiny prints running side by side. Draw the prints or take a photograph and record in a notebook the date and place, ground conditions and other observations. The second project shows you how to make casts of the most interesting footprints.

▲ **Out and about**
Study the tracks that you have found very carefully. What do they tell you about the way the animal that made them moved – did it hop, run or waddle? Use a field guide to animal tracks to help you identify the animals that left them.

YOU WILL NEED

magnifying glass, camera, notebook, pencil, field guide.

Animal tracks

1 When you find a footprint, count the number of toes. Can you see any claws? A fox's paw is rounded, with four toes and claws. Take photos or make drawings of animal tracks you see.

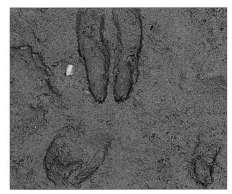

2 Deer have narrow, split hooves with just two toes. They leave deep tracks because they walk with all their weight on their toes, rather than evenly spread throughout their feet.

3 Most birds have long, spindly feet, with either three or four toes. All ducks and some wading birds have webbed feet. The web shows up in the outline of the print.

Footprint cast

1 Find a clear animal track either in sand or dry mud. Remove any loose twigs or leaves around the print. (Remember to wear gloves if you are working in soil.)

2 Look for bird footprints in wet sand or mud. Tracks show the size of the bird that made it and what group of birds it belongs to. Use a field guide to identify the bird that made the print.

3 Bend a strip of card into a ring large enough to fit around the print and secure the card ring with a paper clip. Place the ring over the print.

4 Mix the plaster of Paris with a little water in a bowl, according to the instructions on the packet. Stir the mixture until it is a thick and even paste with no lumps.

5 Carefully spoon enough plaster of Paris on to the print to cover it completely. After 15 minutes the cast will be dry enough for you to pick it up.

6 Use a trowel to prise the cast loose. Carefully peel away the paper ring. Clean up the cast by brushing off any loose soil or sand with a scrubbing brush.

7 Allow the plaster cast to dry for 24 hours. After this you could paint or varnish the cast. Try painting the raised footprint one colour and the background another colour.

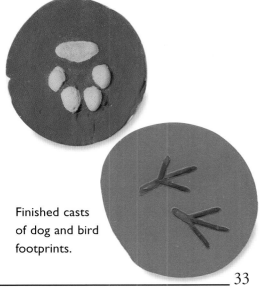

Finished casts of dog and bird footprints.

Searching for insects

▲ Feet tasters

The housefly has taste sensors on its feet. It sucks up its liquid through spongy mouthparts as soon as it lands.

Insects make up three-quarters of all animal species (kinds) on the Earth. Insects are everywhere so they are easy to find. The best place to start is your garden or a local park. If there is a good range of plants, up to 300 species of beetles can be found in a very small area, such as gardens. There may be up to 200 kinds of flies, 90 different bugs and many species of bees, ants, wasps, moths and butterflies.

To identify the species living in a particular area, scientists mark off a square, and search all the places where creatures hide – under leaves, stones and logs, and in tiny crevices in trees. Scientists may leave pitfall traps in the ground, or hang traps in the trees. You can find creatures locally using the type of trap demonstrated in the first project. The second project shows you how to make a simple pooter, that enables you to collect insects without harming them. Wear gloves when handling insects as some may sting or bite. Always take an adult out with you.

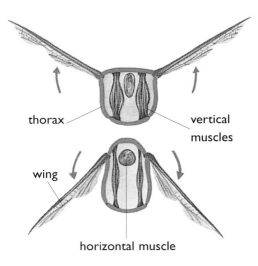

thorax   vertical muscles

wing

horizontal muscle

▲ How insects fly

Insects have no muscles in their wings. Instead the wings are hinged to the insect's thorax. They move up and down as the thorax changes shape. As the roof of the thorax is pulled down, the wings flick up. As the ends of the thorax are pulled in, the wings flick down.

Pitfall trap

1 If you have a garden, ask an adult to show you a place where you can dig a small hole. Use a trowel to dig a hole in damp earth, large enough for the jar to fit in.

2 Place the jar in the hole. Firm the earth back around the sides of the jar with your hands. Put small, fresh leaves in the bottom of the jar for minibeast bait.

3 Place some small stones around the trap and balance a large flat stone or tile on top, to prevent the minibeast trap from filling up with rain. Leave it overnight.

4 In the morning, remove the jar. Place a piece of muslin over the top and secure it with an elastic band. Study any minibeasts you have caught using a magnifying glass.

5 Use a field guide to identify the minibeasts you have caught. When you have finished, remember to release the creatures near to where you found them.

wasp

centipede

▲ **Show a leg**

Centipedes, like insects, are members of the arthropod group. They have many legs, one pair on each body segment. Adult insects, such as this queen wasp, have bodies in three main sections and six legs. Most also have wings.

Make a pooter

YOU WILL NEED

Pitfall trap: gardening gloves, trowel, glass jar, small fresh leaves, small stones, large flat stone or tile, muslin, elastic band, magnifying glass, field guide.

Make a pooter: small plastic bottle, scissors, non-hardening modelling material, wide bendy straws, small piece of muslin, elastic band, sharp pencil.

1 Cut off the bottom of the plastic bottle. Roll out one large and one small ball of modelling material. Flatten out the large ball and mould it over the bottom of the bottle.

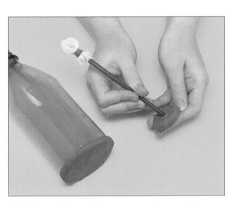

2 To make a filter, cut a short piece of straw. Secure a piece of muslin around the straw with an elastic band. Push the other end through the small lump of modelling material.

3 Fit the filter into the neck of the bottle by moulding the modelling material. Make a hole in the bottom flap with a sharp pencil. Fit a long straw into the hole you have made.

4 Look for a small insect to study. (Big insects would get damaged.) Aim the end of the long straw over the insect. Suck on the short straw to draw the insect safely into the pooter.

5 When you have finished studying your insect, take it back to where you found it. To release the insect, carefully remove the bottom flap and shake the insect out.

What is an insect?

Birds, reptiles and mammals all have internal skeletons to provide a framework for their bodies. Insects are different – they have skeletons on the outside. Their soft body parts are protected by a hard case called an exoskeleton. This forms a waterproof barrier around the insect. It prevents the insect from drying out and air from passing through. Unlike birds and mammals, insects are cold-blooded animals. This means the temperature of an insect's body is about the same as its surroundings. To warm up, an insect basks in the sunshine. When it gets too hot, it moves into the shade.

Insects are fragile. It can be difficult to pick them up and examine them without harming them. When studying insects, use a notebook to record what you see. Write down the date, time, weather conditions and place where you found the insect. Use a field guide to help you make an identification. The projects here show you how to keep a record of the insects that you see. Look at the mouthparts and antennae. Think about the shape of the insect's body. Is it short or long? Does the insect have hard wing cases, or long legs?

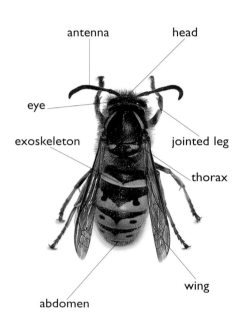

antenna   head

eye

exoskeleton   jointed leg

thorax

wing

abdomen

▲ Wasp sections
The bodies of adult insects have three sections – head, thorax and abdomen. Like this wasp, each section is made of small plates that fit together at flexible joints. The head carries the mouth parts, antennae and eyes. The legs and wings are attached to the thorax. The abdomen contains the reproductive organs and part of the digestive system.

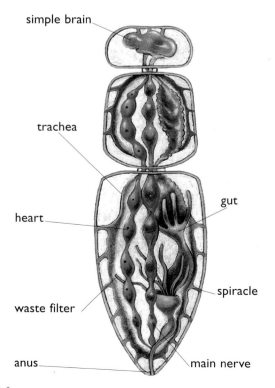

simple brain

trachea

heart

gut

waste filter

spiracle

anus

main nerve

◄ Inside the insect
An insect's internal systems are protected by its hard exoskeleton. This diagram shows the main systems separated out and coloured to make them clear. The nervous system (purple) sends messages from the senses to the brain. In the respiratory system (grey), air enters the body through tiny holes along each side of the insect's body, called spiracles. Pipes called tracheae carry the air to other parts of the body. In the circulatory system (red) several hearts, arranged in a row, pump blood around the body. The digestive system (green, orange) processes food.

Drawing insects

1 Find an insect and use the magnifying glass to study it closely. Start by drawing three ovals to show the head, the thorax and the abdomen of the insect.

2 Can you see the insect's legs? Copy them on your drawing. Now copy the size and shape of the insect's antennae. Draw in the eyes and add the outline of the wings.

3 Now draw any markings that you notice on the insect's body and wings (if it has them). Finish off your drawing by colouring it in as accurately as you can.

Insect survey

1 Find an area of long grass. Wearing gloves, use the tent pegs, a measuring tape and string to mark out a square measuring one metre on each side.

2 What insects can you find inside the square? Use a collecting jar and a magnifying glass to study them. Write down what you have found in a notebook.

3 Now mark out a square metre in a different place. Try an area with flowers or a hedge. You may find aphids and ladybirds on plant stems, and shieldbugs under leaves.

4 Move a fallen log to see what kinds of insects live underneath. Make sure you wear gloves to protect your hands. You may find beetles under logs and woodlice and earwigs under bark.

5 Still wearing gloves, carefully look under some stones. What kinds of creatures prefer this dark, damp habitat? You may find worms, snails, ground beetles or an ants' nest.

Use your field guide to identify your finds. How many different species did you find in each area? Make a chart to record the results of your survey.

Studying insect life

▲ Insect pollination

This wasp is visiting a flower to feed on its sugary nectar. It sucks up the nectar with its tongue to feed the larvae (young) in its nest. As the wasp reaches into the centre of the flower, pollen from the flower rubs off on the insect's body. This is then carried by the wasp to the next flower.

Woods are great places to go insect watching. Trees offer food and shelter from the weather so are an ideal habitat for insects. The number of insects you find may depend on the season. In spring, wild flowers bloom and attract insects. In summer, the woods offer insects sunny clearings and cool shade. Choose a large tree and make a survey of all the insects you can find on a single branch. Make a tree trap to catch insects active at night.

Many insects depend on plants, but many plants depend on insects too. Insects help to pollinate plants by carrying pollen from the same plant to another of its species. Many plants have pink, red or orange flowers because these are the colours that butterflies see well. Other flowers have special markings called nectar guides, leading from the base of the petals. Some show up only in ultraviolet light. Insects such as bees have eyes that are sensitive to this light and they follow these guides to the middle of the flower.

Human vision

Insect vision

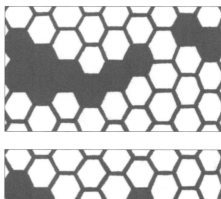

◄ Seeing is believing

Insect vision is very different from ours. Experts think each lens of an insect's compound eye sees a small part of a scene. This gives a mosaic-like view that is built up into a bigger picture. These diagrams compare how we see a moving insect and what experts think an insect sees. An insect can sense tiny movements our eyes would hardly notice because they have many more lenses that are affected.

Make a tree trap

1 Using a pair of sharp scissors, carefully cut the plastic bottle in half widthways. Ask an adult to help you to do this if you find it too difficult.

2 Turn the neck half of the bottle around and push it inside the bottom half. Now tape the two halves of the bottle together using sticky tape.

3 Cut a long piece of string. Loop the string around the open end of the trap and secure it with a knot. Place a small piece of ham inside the trap as insect bait.

4 Carefully tie the trap along the branch of a tree, or hang the trap down underneath the branch. Leave the trap out overnight. Go back the next morning to check it.

5 Use your field guide to identify the insects that you have caught. Record your findings in a notebook. Release the insects when you have identified them.

Life on a branch

1 Spread out the white sheet below a branch. Shake the branch to dislodge the insects on to the sheet. If the branch is high, tap it with a stick. Be sure not to damage the tree.

2 Sweep the insects that drop on to the sheet into collecting jars for you to study. Use a paintbrush to carefully transfer the insects without harming them.

Use a field guide to identify the insects. Try surveying another type of tree. Make a chart, as above, to show the different species found on the different trees.

Insects in disguise

Most insects try to escape from predators by flying away. But it is even better not to be seen at all. Insects that hunt other creatures also need to be invisible to creep up unnoticed on their prey. Many insects have special colours and patterns on their bodies to help them look like leaves, seeds, twigs or stones. These natural disguises are known as camouflage.

Stick insects change their body colour to match their surroundings and so remain hidden almost anywhere. Their long slender bodies and stick-like legs make them hard to see among twigs and leaves. Stick insects are easy to look after at home. You can buy them at some pet shops. Try the test opposite to find out more about camouflage.

You could look outside for ways in which insects disguise themselves. The last project shows you how to attract insects such as butterflies and wasps by planting flowers and herbs. Remember to ask permission from an adult before you start.

▲ **Hidden hunter**
Insects are attracted by the bright colours and sweet scent of flowers. This wasp is almost the same colour as the flower it is feeding on.

▲ **Prickles and bristles**
A pair of giant prickly leaf insects with the green female (*right*) and the smaller male (*left*). The wings of the male are folded along its back. The safest way to pick up leaf or stick insects is by placing your fingers on each side of the body.

YOU WILL NEED

Camouflage test: scissors, light and dark green paper, two cardboard boxes, sticky tape, stick insects, paintbrush, privet or ivy leaves, kitchen paper, muslin, non-hardening modelling material, notebook, coloured pencils.

Rearing stick insects: earth, small tank or large jar, privet or ivy leaves, glass of water, sticks, stick insects, kitchen paper.

Plant a window box: gardening gloves, window box or large tub, earth, compost (optional), packet of wild flower seeds, watering can, notebook, pencil, field guide.

Camouflage test

1 Cut pieces of coloured paper to line the insides of the cardboard boxes. Make one box light green and the other dark green. Attach the paper with sticky tape.

2 Transfer your stick insects with a paintbrush to the light green box. Add leaves and damp kitchen paper. Cover with muslin weighted at the corners with modelling material.

3 Leave the box in a light place for a day. Record the insects' colour with coloured pencils. Put the insects in the darker box. After a day, check to see if they have changed colour.

Rearing stick insects

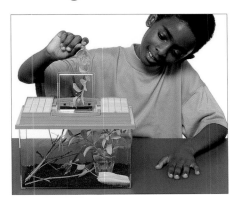

1 Put a layer of earth in the bottom of a tank or a large jar with a tight-fitting lid with small air holes. Add privet or ivy leaves in a glass of water, some sticks and your stick insects.

2 Put some wet kitchen paper in a corner so that the insects have enough moisture. Remember to replace the paper regularly. Ask the pet shop if your insects need anything else.

Plant a window box

1 Wearing gloves, fill a window box or large tub with earth. You could add some compost to the earth and mix it in. The container should be about three-quarters full of earth.

2 Scatter wild flower seeds over the soil. You can buy seeds such as daisy and bird's-foot trefoil at a nursery. Do not dig up wild plants. Cover the seeds with more earth.

3 The seedlings will come up in a few weeks. Water the young plants regularly. As the plants grow, record in your notebook which insects visit and feed on them.

Insects to watch

As insects eat they leave behind damaged plants and other signs of feeding. Sometimes these signs are easier to spot than the insects themselves. Look in a small area, such as a fallen log, a shrub or a bush. Hundreds of insects will be near, but most are small and wary. Discover the eating habits and preferences of different insects in the first project.

Look for freshwater insects such as beetles and bugs in ponds or streams. Spring and summer are good times to look, because the young insects turn into adults at these times. You could even make a small pool for insects in your garden. Ask a responsible adult if you may dig the pond. To catch water insects you will need a net, which you can make easily yourself. When you catch insects at the pond, take an adult with you for safety. Approach the water quietly to disturb the wildlife as little as possible. Different insects live in various places in the pond or stream. Some live near the surface, while others swim near the bottom. Gently lift up stones and pebbles to find the creatures that lurk on the underside. Always replace them carefully so that you disturb the habitat as little as possible.

▲ **Mmm, my favourite ...**
Most plant-eating insects prefer one particular food and may eat only a part of that food plant. Some insects leave ragged holes in leaves. Aphids and other bugs leave brown or yellow lines on crops when they suck out the sap.

Food samples

YOU WILL NEED

stiff card, pair of compasses and pencil, scissors, four garden sticks, small samples of food (such as jam, meat, cheese and fruit), notebook, field guide.

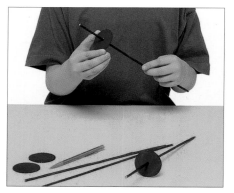

1 Make four circles on the card with the compasses. Cut them out. Use the point of the compasses or a pencil to make holes in the centres of the circles. Push the sticks through the holes.

2 Plant the sticks in the ground. Push the food samples on the sticks, so they rest on the circles. Do insects prefer certain foods? Are there more insects around at different times of day?

Insect pool

1 Wear gloves when you are making your insect pool. Dig a hollow in the ground with the trowel. The hole should be big enough to fit an old plastic bowl inside.

2 Place the bowl in the hollow and press it down firmly. Spread gravel on the bottom and put in the water plants. Place stones arond the edge of the bowl and inside it.

3 Then fill the bowl with water, using a watering can. Your pool is now finished and ready for occupation. Insects and other animal life will soon be attracted to the pool.

Make a pond net

YOU WILL NEED

Insect pool: gardening gloves, trowel, plastic bowl, gravel, water plants, large stones, watering can.

Make a pond net: wire, thin sock, pliers, long pole or broom handle, jubilee clip from a hardware shop, screwdriver, jug, empty plastic ice-cream container, magnifying glass, field guide.

1 Begin your pond net by threading wire in and out through the top of a thin sock. You may need to use a pair of pliers to bend the wire into a circle.

2 Use the pair of pliers to twist the ends of the wire together to make the net secure. Ask an adult to help if you need to. Now position the net at the end of a long pole.

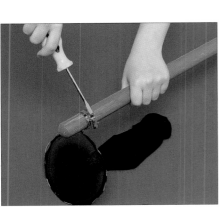

3 Carefully thread the jubilee clip over the pole and push the twisted wires under the clip, as shown above. Tighten the clip using a screwdriver. Ask an adult to help you do this.

4 Down at the pond, capture insects by sweeping your net gently through the water. Lightly tap the stems of plants to knock other insects into your net.

5 Empty a jug of pond water into a container. Empty your net into it. Study the creatures you have caught. Tip the water and creatures back into the pond when you have finished.

Moths and butterflies

All butterflies and moths go through a metamorphosis (change). They start as caterpillars then, as pupae, encase themselves in a cocoon, where a remarkable change takes place and they finally emerge as adults. Caterpillars feed on leafy plants, such as grasses and nettles. Adult moths and butterflies gather on plants with nectar-bearing flowers. As you will see from the projects here, bright lights and a mixture of fruit and sugar will bring moths fluttering.

Some butterflies have wings with warning colours. The markings tell predators that they are poisonous to eat. Other butterflies are harmless, but mimic (copy) poisonous species. Their colours fool predators into avoiding them as well. The best way to attract butterflies is to plant a butterfly garden. Choose plants that bloom at various times of the year.

▲ Beating around the bush
The sweet-smelling purple buddleia is a popular plant with butterflies and so has gained the nickname butterfly bush. Butterflies attracted to buddleia include small tortoiseshells (*shown here*), peacocks, painted ladies, commas and red admirals.

▲ Antennae ID
You can tell a butterfly from a moth by looking at the antennae (feelers). Many butterflies have antennae with clubbed tips, like this Swallowdale. Moths' antennae vary but most are straight or feathered.

Torchlight attraction

1 Wearing gloves, dig a small hole in the garden with a trowel. Do this in daylight and remember to ask an adult's permission first before you start to dig.

2 Check that your torch fits inside the hole. At dusk turn on the torch and put it inside the hole. Fill any gaps with earth to hold the torch securely in position.

3 Step back and watch the moths flutter around the light. You could try taking flash photographs of the insects with a camera. How did your photos turn out?

Sweet moth feast

1 Begin by measuring out about 500g of brown sugar with a spoon into your scales or a measuring bowl. Pour the measured sugar into your mixing bowl.

2 Add the overripe fruit to the mixing bowl and mash it with a fork. Keep mashing until the fruit has become a pulp. Add some warm water until the mixture becomes runny.

3 Paint the mixture on to a tree trunk or fence post. Return when it is dark. Take a torch to help you see the moths feeding and a field guide to help you to identify them.

Butterfly garden

YOU WILL NEED

Torchlight attraction: gardening gloves, trowel, small torch, camera.

Sweet moth feast: brown sugar, spoon, weighing scales, mixing bowl, soft over-ripe fruit, fork, warm water, paintbrush, torch, field guide.

Butterfly garden: seeds or young plants, gloves, trowel, rake, watering can, notebook, pencil, field guide.

1 First you need to grow some plants from seed – or buy young plants. Wearing a pair of gloves, dig over your chosen patch of earth with a trowel.

2 Break up any large clods of earth with a rake or trowel. Now start to rake over the top of your plot so that the earth is evenly spread and crumbly.

3 Dig several small holes for your plants with the trowel. Place the plants in the holes and press the earth down firmly with gloved hands around the base of each plant.

4 Water the plants well. They will need to be watered regularly through the spring and summer. The sun will scorch wet leaves during the day, so water your plants at dusk.

5 Record which butterflies you see visiting your flowers. A field guide will help you to identify them. Which species prefer which flowers? And which is the most popular plant?

Watching a caterpillar grow

These projects show you how to prepare a home for caterpillars. Look for caterpillars on plants where you see half-eaten leaves – they may be hiding on the undersides. Take some of these leaves with the caterpillars you find. Use a field guide to identify the species you have found and which plants they prefer. Try not to touch caterpillars directly with your fingers, as some species may sting. Pick them up with a paintbrush, or encourage them to climb on to a leaf. Carry them in a jar. At home, keep caterpillars out of direct sunlight, in a moist, cool place. Try not to disturb them. Clean the box regularly and replace old leaves with fresh ones.

YOU WILL NEED

scissors, cardboard box, strong sticky tape, muslin or netting, non-hardening modelling material, rubber gloves, fresh leaves, kitchen paper, collecting jar containing caterpillars, ruler, pencil, notebook, field guide, coloured pencils.

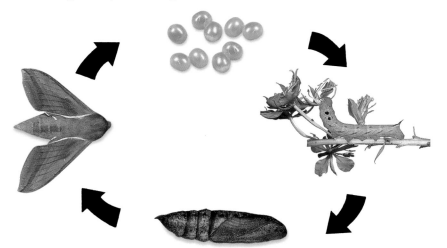

◄ Complete metamorphosis
When butterflies, moths, ants and bees change during their lives, it is called complete metamorphosis. The life cycle of the elephant hawk moth shown here has four separate stages. The moth begins life as an egg. The egg hatches out a caterpillar, which spends almost all of its time feeding. When the caterpillar is fully grown, it burrows into the ground and sheds its skin to reveal a pupa, a stage at which the larva changes into the adult insect while cocooned in a protective case. Finally the case splits and the adult moth emerges.

Keeping caterpillars

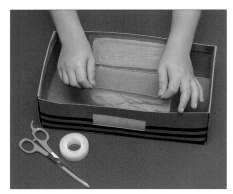

1 Cut holes in the sides of the box for windows. Using strong sticky tape, stick pieces of muslin or netting over the windows to cover them securely.

2 Now cut a large piece of muslin to make the cage lid. Weight the corners of the muslin lid down with modelling material to prevent the caterpillars from escaping.

3 Wearing a pair of gloves, put some fresh leaves inside the box. Make sure that they are from a plant your caterpillars eat. Be sure to provide fresh leaves daily.

4 Put some damp kitchen paper in a corner of the box to provide moisture. Carefully transfer your caterpillars from the collecting jar to the box. Cover with the lid.

5 Check your caterpillars every day and replace the damp kitchen paper. Record how much they eat and how big they are. Remember to replace the leaves daily.

6 Watch how your caterpillars feed and move about on the leaves. Record the dates when you see them moulting (shedding skin). How many times did they shed their skins?

7 When it has finished growing, the caterpillar will change into a pupa, or chrysalis. It will attach itself to the stem of a food plant and form a new skin. Make a note of the date.

8 Check your pupa every day and write down the date when you see the case splitting. Compare your two dates. How long did the insect spend as a pupa?

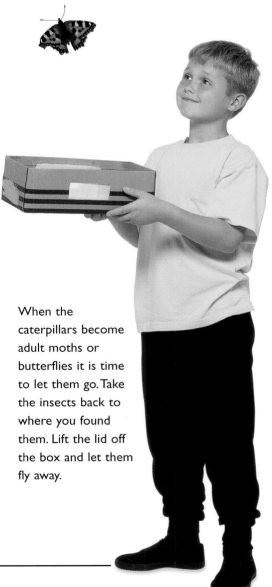

9 You will see a butterfly or moth struggle out of the old skin. The insect rests and pumps blood into its crumpled wings to straighten them out before flying off.

June – July	caterpillar feeds	
end July		pupa forms
mid-August		butterfly emerges

Keep a chart of the life cycles of your insects.

When the caterpillars become adult moths or butterflies it is time to let them go. Take the insects back to where you found them. Lift the lid off the box and let them fly away.

Crawling colonies

Unlike most insects, ants live in colonies. They are known as social insects as opposed to solitary insects. Ants are different to flying insects, such as butterflies and bees, yet they behave in a similar way. An ant colony is like an underground city with millions of insects, each with its own role to play. Queen ants (of which there may be several in one nest) lay eggs. Undeveloped females called workers carry out the essential tasks of the colony. They scurry around, searching for food and bring it to the nest.

The key to the smooth running of the colony is good communication. Ants cannot see well, so they communicate by touch and smell. When two ants meet, they touch antennae (feelers). When an ant finds a food source, it hurries back to the nest, pressing its body on to the ground as it runs. This leaves a trail of scent, which the other ants can follow to reach the food.

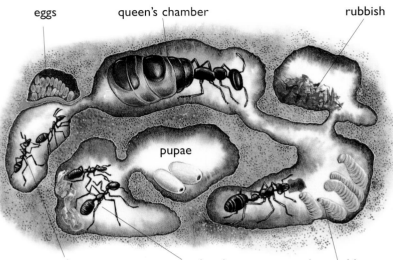

eggs   queen's chamber   rubbish

pupae

workers   young ants hatch   worker and larvae

▲ Inside an ants' nest

Ants' nests are usually underground. A nest has many chambers, or rooms, and passages. Different chambers contain the eggs, larvae (young), pupae and the queen. Other chambers are used to store food and rubbish. Worker ants alter the temperature of the nest by opening or closing passages.

YOU WILL NEED
gardening gloves, peeled ripe fruit, piece of paper, magnifying glass.

Watching ant trails

1 Wearing gloves, find a trail of ants. Follow the trail to find out where the ants are going. Does the trail lead to food? Rub out part of the trail and see what happens.

2 Now put fruit down on a piece of paper near the trail of ants. The paper will make it easier to see the ants. When the workers find the fruit, watch to see what happens.

3 Once an ant has laid a scent trail to the fruit, others will follow. Move the fruit to another part of the paper. What happens next? Do the ants go straight to the new food site?

Make an ant home

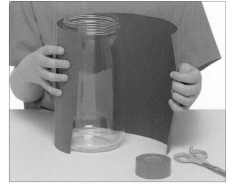

1 Measure and cut a piece of dark-coloured paper that is large enough to fit around the jar. Fix the paper in position around the jar with sticky tape.

2 Wearing a pair of gloves, use the trowel to fill the jar with earth until the jar is almost full. Carefully place a few leaves on top of the earth.

3 Capture some garden ants using a paintbrush and collecting jar. Let the ants crawl on to the paintbrush. Then tap the jar so that the ants fall in. Transfer the ants to their new home.

4 Feed your ants with a piece of ripe fruit or jam. Some damp kitchen paper will provide moisture. Feed your ants daily and refresh the leaves and moist paper regularly.

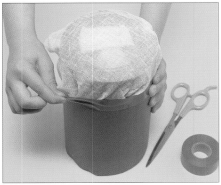

5 Cover the top of the jar with a piece of muslin, so that the ants cannot escape. Secure the muslin with sticky tape. Keep your ant home in a cool place.

6 After a few days, remove the sticky tape and lift the paper to observe your ant home. There will now be winding tunnels, built by the ants, against the sides of the jar.

If you have caught a queen ant, you may see the workers tending eggs or larvae in special chambers.

Discovering birds

There are birds living in all areas of the world. They inhabit icy polar regions, tropical wet rainforests and scorching hot deserts. Birds are also found in crowded cities, on high mountains and remote islands.

Birds vary in size. The tiny hummingbird of Cuba is no larger than a bumblebee. The African ostrich, at the other extreme, stands 2.5m high. Birds are warm-blooded creatures like mammals, but they lay eggs, as reptiles and amphibians do. Unlike other animals, birds' bodies are covered with strong, lightweight feathers. These help birds to fly, although there are a few species (kinds) that cannot fly.

There are more than 8,600 different species of birds. Scientist divide all these birds into groups called orders. The 28 bird orders are divided into smaller groups, called families, and each family contains several species. Species in the same family tend to have a similar body shape, which makes them suited to a certain way of life. For example, ducks have wide bodies and webbed feet to help them move through water.

The largest bird species often live the longest. Giant albatrosses can live for 80 years. Small songbird species, such as blue tits and sparrows, may live for just one year.

skull
nostril
neck
backbone
keel
wingbone
ribcage
ankle
toe

▲ Body shape
Birds have a basic body shape that varies in size and colour according to species. All birds have a beak, instead of jaws with teeth, and scaly legs and feet. Flying birds have a skeleton that is geared for efficient flight. Powerful wings and a feathered tail help with stability and steering. The wings and legs are arranged close to the centre of the body, to help with balance.

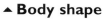

left eye socket

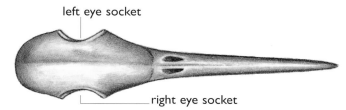

right eye socket

▲ Field of vision for a woodcock
A woodcock eats earthworms and insects. It does not need to spot prey like an owl does but must look out for enemies. Its eyes are on the sides of its head. This enables it to see all around itself.

YOU WILL NEED

Looking at diving birds: field guide, stopwatch or watch with a second hand, notebook, pen, drawing pad, coloured pencils.
Drawing birds: drawing pad, pen and pencils, notebook.

Looking at diving birds

1 Choose a pond or lake for bird-watching. See where different species feed. Notice where they dive and reappear. Use a field guide to help you to identify species.

2 Now find out how long the different birds spend under the water. Use your stopwatch to time their dives. Do they feed under water, or bring food to the surface?

3 Record the times in your notebook. Which bird stays under water for the longest time? Do you think that this is affected by the depth of the water?

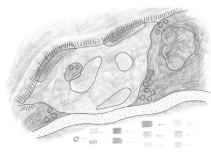
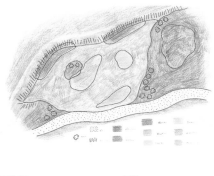

4 In your notebook, make a rough map of the pond or lake. When you get home, do a neater version and colour it in. Show vegetation such as grass or reeds.

5 On your map, use different coloured pencils to mark where various species of birds swim and feed. Remember to draw a key to explain which bird each colour represents.

Drawing birds

1 You do not have to be a great artist to draw birds. Study the shape of the bird. Notice how long the neck is. Start with simple ovals for the head and body.

2 Look at the shape of the bird's beak, and at its neck and tail. If you can see the legs, how long are they? Can you see the feet? Add these details to your drawing.

Now add a pair of wings and other details, such as the face and tail. Make notes about the bird's colouring. so that you can colour your drawing in later.

Bird-watching

Birds are among the easiest animals to spot and study from your home or school. To see a wider range of species (kinds), you could try bird-watching in a local park, pond or woodland area. Always take an adult with you. Birds are shy creatures with sharp eyesight and hearing. They are always on the lookout for enemies, so keep very quiet and still when bird-watching. If you make yourself a hide, like the one shown, bird-watching will be much easier.

> ### YOU WILL NEED
>
> **Using binoculars:** binoculars.
> **Build a hide:** eight short canes or poles, six longer canes, string, scissors, canvas or tarpaulin, safety pins, four tent pegs, leaves and twigs, lightweight binoculars.

Using binoculars

1 Lightweight binoculars are very useful on bird-watching trips. Remove them from the case and hang them around your neck so you are ready to use them.

2 When you see a bird, do not look down, or you may lose sight of it. Keep watching it, and slowly raise the binoculars to your eyes. Try to avoid sudden movements.

3 Now adjust the focusing wheel on your binoculars to bring the bird into focus. You may find this difficult to do at first, but it will become easier with practice.

Build a hide

1 You will need a friend to help you. Lay four short canes on the ground in a square. Tie the ends with string. Make another square the same size, to form the roof.

2 Get your friend to stand inside the base. Your friend should hold the roof in position while you tie four long canes to the base and roof to form the sides.

3 Now strengthen the structure of your hide. Add two long canes to make cross-pieces on opposite sides of the hide. Tie the canes in place with string.

4 Drape your hide with the canvas or tarpaulin. Add a smaller piece for the roof. Fasten the edges with safety pins. For extra security, fix the base to the ground with tent pegs.

5 Now cover the cloth with some leaves and twigs. These will camouflage your hide, so that it will blend in with the woods and will be less obvious to birds.

6 Once inside the hide, look out through the gaps in the seams, between the safety pins. Try using your binoculars. Keep still and quiet, and birds will soon approach.

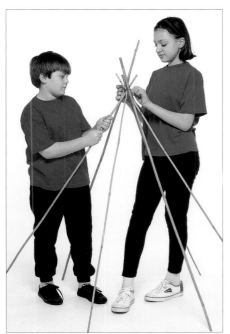

Camouflage the tipi with leaves and twigs. Leave a gap to look through the cover with your binoculars.

A tipi is another, simpler kind of hide. You will need four to six canes, string, a tarpaulin, safety pins and possibly tent pegs. Fan out the canes to form a pyramid shape and tie the top ends with string. Drape the tarpaulin over this and fasten it with safety pins.

Listening to birds

The voices of singing birds that seem beautiful to us often have many meanings. A bird's song identifies what species (kind) it is as well as each bird as an individual. Male birds sing to establish their own territories. A territory is a patch of ground where the birds intend to breed or feed. In Antarctica, a parent penguin finds its chick among thousands of other chicks by its cry. Birds also call to warn of danger and to attract a mate. Birds that flock together use contact calls to keep in a tight group.

You can make a birdbath for the birds visiting your garden in the first project. Listening to birdsong is a good way of identifying birds. The best times of the day to listen to birds are dawn and dusk, when they sing the loudest. It is fun to make recordings of the different bird songs that you come across. Use a portable tape recorder with a long lead, so that you can position the microphone farther away. Tape the microphone to a stick, so that the sounds of your hands will not be recorded. Headphones allow you to check what you are recording. To achieve even better results, make yourself a sound reflector, as shown in the third project.

▲ Hooters of the night
An owl's night-time hooting is a well-recognized sound. Owls have excellent eyesight which makes them good hunters in the dark. Some have flat disc-shaped faces to help direct sound into the ears at the sides of the head.

YOU WILL NEED

trowel, rubber gloves, large dish or old dustbin lid, stones, bucket of water.

Build a bird-bath

1 Use your trowel to dig a hollow in the earth. It should be big enough to fit your dustbin lid or dish. Place the dish in the hollow and press it down firmly, making sure it is flat.

2 Now place a few large stones in your dustbin lid or dish. Birds coming to your garden will use these stones to stand on to get in and out of your bird-bath.

3 Pour water into the bath, to a depth of about 10–15cm. The tops of the stones should stick up above the water, so that birds can spot them and land on them easily.

YOU WILL NEED

Taping birdsong: portable tape recorder, microphone and headphones, blank cassette tapes, notebook, pencil, camping mat, field guide.

Sound reflector: old umbrella, foil, sticky tape, tape recorder, microphone and headphones, blank cassette tape.

Taping birdsong

I Become familiar with the songs of birds that live in your area by listening to recordings on CD or cassette tape. You can borrow these from your local library.

2 Outside, position yourself behind a tree or bush, if possible. Set up the microphone on a long lead by a bird-table, or near a perch where you see a bird singing.

3 To record, press the record and pause buttons, releasing the pause button when you want to record. Listen with headphones and also note down the time, place and weather.

When you get home, listen to the calls you have recorded very carefully. Most field guides give details of bird-calls and will be able to help you to identify the songs.

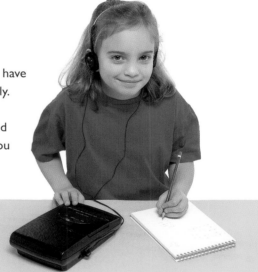

Sound reflector

I Cover the inside of an old umbrella with sheets of foil. Carefully bend the foil over the edges of the umbrella and tape it down securely with sticky tape.

2 Fix the mike to the stem of the umbrella, with the mike head pointing towards the shade. Try the mike in different positions – about 15–20cm away from the shade.

3 Set up your reflector where birds are singing. The reflector will channel sounds and amplify them (make them louder). Give birds time to get used to this strange object.

Birds' nests

Nests are warm, safe places where birds lay eggs and where the nestlings (baby birds) develop after they have hatched. Birds do not sleep in their nests at night. Instead, they roost on perches in sheltered places such as hedges and trees.

Constructing the nest is usually the female's job. The first step is to choose a good site. Then the materials are gathered. Twigs, leaves, feathers, moss, wool and mud are all used by various birds. The nest-building bird pushes the materials into place and hollows out the inside with her body. The finished nest may be lined with soft materials such as feathers to protect the eggs.

Nesting birds are fascinating to study. Attract birds into your garden and help them to nest and raise their young by building a nesting box in early spring. You may see birds fly by with nesting materials in their beaks, looking for a place to build. Many birds build their nests wedged in the forks of tree branches. Nest-building uses up a lot of time and energy. It may take between a week and a month, yet most nests last for just one breeding season, and are ruined by winter weather.

▲ Nesting materials

In spring, try hanging nesting material from branches or a windowsill. You can use wool, string, grass, moss and feathers. You could also try paper tissue, straw or animal hair. Different bird species like different materials. Keep a look-out to see which materials are chosen by various birds.

Template for nesting box

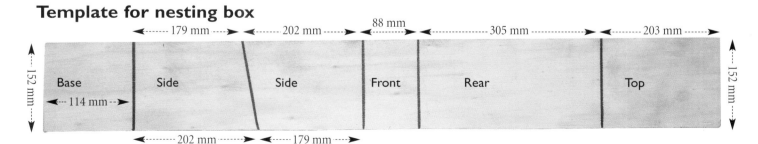

| Base | Side | Side | Front | Rear | Top |

179 mm, 202 mm, 88 mm, 305 mm, 203 mm, 152 mm, 114 mm, 202 mm, 179 mm, 152 mm

Use 15mm thick pine or plywood. Ask an adult to cut pieces to the sizes and shapes shown above.

Build a nesting box

YOU WILL NEED

wood (cut into pieces by an adult as shown), wood glue, hammer, nails or panel pins, pencil, strip of sacking or rubber (for the hinge), varnish, brush.

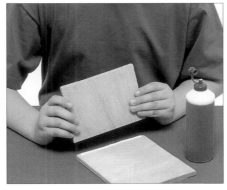

1 When all the pieces of wood have been cut by an adult, arrange them in position to make sure that they all fit properly. Glue the low front of the box to the base.

2 Now add one of the side pieces to the base of your nesting box. Glue it in place. Next add the other side piece to the opposite edge of the base and glue that into position, as well.

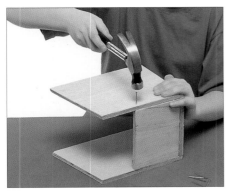

3 Nail all the pieces together. Take great care with the hammer. You could ask an adult to help. Place the box in the middle of the rear board, and draw around it in pencil.

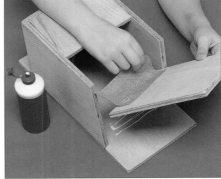

4 Using your pencil guidelines, nail the rear board to the box. Add the roof by gluing and nailing on the sacking hinge. Now your nesting box is ready to use.

5 Your nesting box will last much longer if you give it a coat of varnish inside and out to protect it. Leave the box overnight to let the varnish dry completely.

Nail your box to a tree, shed or post, about 2m from the ground. Face the box away from any direct sunlight, as this may harm very young birds.

Feed the birds

Put bird food out in a safe place and you will discover one of the best ways of studying birds close up. You can make your own bird cake, such as the one here, and put out kitchen scraps such as stale breadcrumbs, cheese, fruit, cooked rice or pasta, uncooked pastry and bacon rind. Birds will really appreciate these titbits, particularly in cold weather, when the ground is hard to peck at for worms and trees are bare of fruit and berries. Count how many different kinds of birds visit. Also, notice which species (kinds) prefer each kind of food. Note down the date, time and weather when you first see a new species. Do the birds feed quietly together, or do they fight over scraps?

▲ Winter feed
Fruit is an important food for many birds, particularly in winter. Garden birds such as thrushes and blackbirds will peck at apples, leaving large, irregular holes.

◀ Shells and nuts
Look out for nut shells gnawed by animals. Squirrels and mice leave neat holes and teethmarks. Birds leave peck-marks or jagged edges or crack nuts in half, such as the top two nuts here. Song thrushes feed on snails. They smash the shell against a stone. The stone is known as the thrush's anvil. You may be lucky and find shell remains beside a stone.

Make a bird cake

1 Soften the fat on a radiator or get an adult to help you melt it in a pan. Mix the nuts, oatmeal and crumbs in a bowl. Add the fat and mix together.

2 Cut a long piece of string. Tie a really big knot in one end. Put the string into the cup so that the knotted end is at the bottom, and spoon the mixture into the cup.

3 Ensure that the end of the string comes out through the middle of the mixture. When the mixture is set, pull the string to remove the cake. Hang it on a tree branch or windowsill.

Build a bird table

1 Lay the wooden strips along the edges of your plywood board, as shown. Now glue the strips of wood into position, so that the ends fit together neatly.

2 When the glue is dry, turn the board over. Carefully hammer nails through it into the strips. If you find using a hammer difficult, you could ask an adult to help you to do this.

3 Paint the top surface of your bird table with a coat of varnish, to make it waterproof. When this coat is dry, turn the table over and coat the underside too.

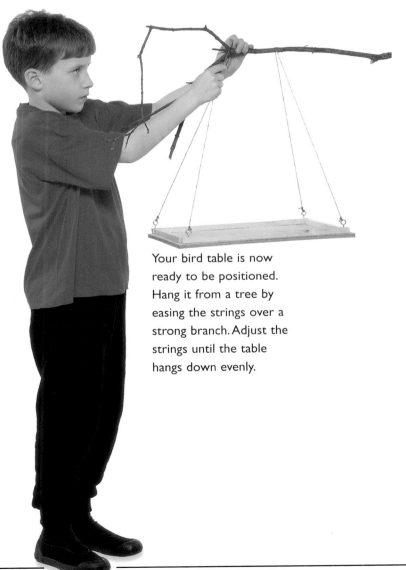

Your bird table is now ready to be positioned. Hang it from a tree by easing the strings over a strong branch. Adjust the strings until the table hangs down evenly.

4 Screw eye-hooks into the strips at the four corners of the table. Now cut two pieces of string about 30cm long. Tie the ends of the strings to the hooks.

Bird travel and flight

Many birds travel vast distances each year. They may travel to escape the chill of winter, to find food or a safe nesting site. Departure is often triggered by the shortening daylight hours of autumn. In spring, the birds travel back again. These journeys are called migrations. Many species (kinds) do not feed while they travel, so must fatten up before they leave. Migrating birds face many dangers. They may get lost in storms or be killed by predators. Thousands die of hunger, thirst and exhaustion.

Flying takes up a lot of energy but has many advantages for birds. Hovering uses the most energy of all. However, birds are able to save their energy by gliding on air currents. Large birds soar upwards into air currents with their wings outstretched to trap as much air as possible. Making your own aerofoil in the project opposite shows you how the shape of a wing produces lift. Then build a spiral model to see how birds circle in warm air currents without flapping their wings.

▲ Lift and flight

A bird's wing is slightly curved at the top, and flatter underneath. A shape like this that is designed to provide uplift in flight is called an aerofoil. As the bird moves through the air, the curved shape makes the air travel faster over the wing than beneath it. This makes an area of low air pressure above the wing, which allows the bird to rise. Aircraft are able to fly because their wings are a similar shape to a bird's wings.

Migration routes

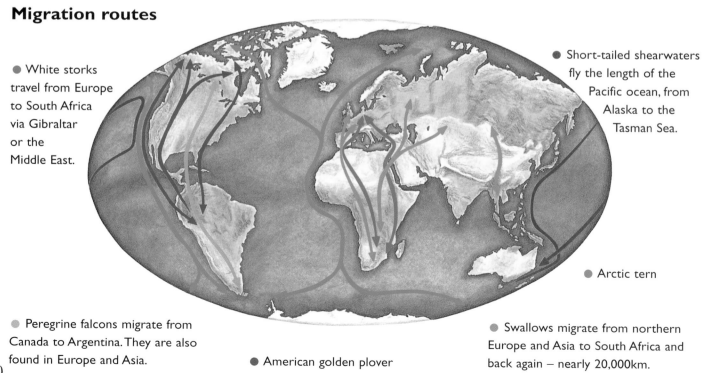

● White storks travel from Europe to South Africa via Gibraltar or the Middle East.

● Short-tailed shearwaters fly the length of the Pacific ocean, from Alaska to the Tasman Sea.

● Arctic tern

● Peregrine falcons migrate from Canada to Argentina. They are also found in Europe and Asia.

● American golden plover

● Swallows migrate from northern Europe and Asia to South Africa and back again – nearly 20,000km.

How a wing works

1 Cut a strip of paper about 30cm long. Glue the ends together firmly. When the glue is dry, bend the paper into a wing shape, curved on top and flat underneath.

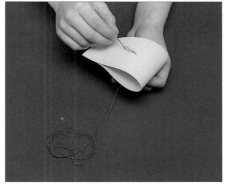

2 Mark the centre of the wing. Thread a long piece of cotton on to a needle and push it through the centre of the wing. Gently pull the aerofoil down the thread.

3 Now get a friend to hold the thread taut. Blow hard against the curved edge of the aerofoil, and watch the wing rise up the thread – just as an aeroplane or a bird's wing lifts.

Soaring spiral

YOU WILL NEED

How a wing works: paper, scissors, glue, pencil, needle, thread.

Soaring spiral: thick paper, pair of compasses, pencil, coloured pencils/felt-tipped pens, scissors, pencil with rubber on end, cotton reel, pin, thimble.

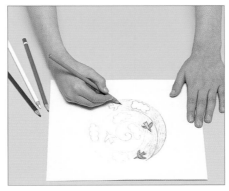

1 Use a pair of compasses and a pencil to draw a circle on a piece of paper. Now draw and colour in a spiral shape with buzzards (or other birds) flying around it.

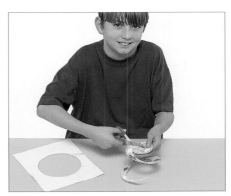

2 Carefully cut out the decorated paper spiral. Use a pencil to make the hole left in the centre of the spiral by your compasses big enough to fit over the thimble.

3 Fit the pencil point into the cotton reel. Put the pin in the rubber. Push the thimble through the hole in the paper spiral, so that it sits over the thimble. Balance the thimble on the pin.

4 Stand your model on a radiator. Now watch the buzzards circling around in the warm air currents rising from the radiator. Your model must be well-balanced to work properly.

Glossary

A

antenna The plural of antenna is antennae. These are the long jointed structures found on the head of many invertebrates and are used as feelers and also to smell.

artificial Describes something that is not created as part of a natural process or with naturally occurring materials.

attrition The rubbing together and wearing down of particles carried by wind, water or ice.

B

bacteria Simple living organisms, usually consisting of single cells. Many bacteria are parasites and cause disease.

burrowing animals Animals that dig holes or tunnels underground, most often to live in.

C

camouflage The adoption of colours, patterns, and texture in order to merge with the environment and so be hidden or disguised.

carbon dioxide A colourless, odourless gas containing the elements carbon and oxygen, which is a part of air.

caterpillar The larva of a butterfly or moth.

chlorophyll The green pigment of plants that absorbs light energy from the Sun.

climate The typical weather pattern of an area.

cocoon A silky, protective envelope, made by silkworms and other insect larvae, to protect the developing pupa.

cold-blooded Animals, such as insects, whose body temperature is the same as their surroundings.

colony A large number of animals or insects belonging to the same species, such as ants, living together in a small area.

D

deciduous Describes trees and shrubs that lose their leaves at the end of each growing season.

decomposers The tiny living creatures, such as microscopic bacteria, fungi, woodlice, mites and small insects, that break down decomposing material into its nutrients.

decomposition The process whereby matter, such as leaves, bark, and dead insects and animals, decays or rots.

density A measure of how tightly or loosely the matter in a substance is packed together.

E

ecosystem A community of living things that interact with each other and their surroundings.

environment The external conditions in which people, animals and plants live on Earth.

Equator The imaginary circle around the middle of the Earth, between the Northern and Southern Hemispheres, where day and night are equal in length, and the climate is hot.

erosion The gradual wearing away of the land by agents of erosion, such as ice, rain, wind and waves.

evaporation The process by which something turns from liquid to vapour.

evergreen Describes plants that bear leaves all the year round.

exoskeleton Outer skeleton – the hard case that protects an insect's soft body parts.

F

felling Cutting down of trees.

fertilization The act or process of the male part of a plant, or a male animal, that enables a female's seed, egg or eggs to produce young.

friction The force caused by two surfaces rubbing together. This results in the slowing down of movement and heat being produced.

G
germination The point at which a plant seed, or an egg in an animal, is fertilized and begins to grow.

H
habitat The natural home of an animal or plant.
hemispheres The top and bottom halves of the Earth, separated by the Equator.
hibernation A period when many animals save energy by remaining inactive. Animals hybernate in order to survive the winter.

I
invertebrate Any animal that does not have a backbone, for example, insects, worms, snails and jellyfish.

K
keratin The substance found in birds' feathers and claws and humans' hair and nails.

L
larva The immature stage in the life of many insects, amphibians and fish.

M
metamorphosis Change, as in the life cycles of some animals, that involves a complete change of form, appearance, and other characteristics.
migration The movement of animals and birds from one area to another, usually over great distances, due to a change in the seasons.
mineral A naturally occurring substance that is found in rocks.
mould A kind of fungus in the form of a woolly growth that is often found on rotten food.

N
nesting Building and occupying nests by birds.
nestlings Baby birds.

O
organism Any living thing, such as a plant or animal, that is capable of growth and reproducing itself.
osmosis The movement of a solvent, such as water, through cell walls, from a more dilute solution to a more concentrated one.

P
photosynthesis The process by which plants make food using energy from sunlight.
plumage The feathers of a bird.
pollination The transfer of pollen by plants to achieve fertilization.
predators Animals that prey on (hunt and kill) other animals for food.
pupa Inactive stage in the life cycle of many insects, such as butterflies and moths.

S
savanna Tropical grassland with drought-resistant trees, most commonly found in Africa.

sediment Solid particles of rock or other material.
solution A mixture of something solid and a liquid into which it has been completely dissolved.
species A group of animals or plants that share similar characteristics and can breed successfully together.

T
territory An area of ground where birds and animals tend to feed.
thermometer An instrument for measuring temperature.
thorax The part of an insect's body between the head and the abdomen, which bears the wings and legs.
tropics Area close to the Equator, between the tropic of Cancer and the tropic of Capricorn.

V
vegetation The plants of a particular area. The plants may be of the same or different species, depending on the climate and soil conditions.

Index